# Roger Ravencraft

# AFTER THE PANDEMIC

How Coronavirus Will Change
the Way We Live, Forever.

# TABLE OF CONTENTS

"*It is not the strongest of the species that survives, nor the most intelligent that survives. It is the one that is most adaptable to change*"

 **CHARLES DARWIN**

# Introduction

## Survival of the Fittest

When Charles Darwin first introduced his philosophies and ideas to the world, they weren't necessarily met with utmost glee and jubilation. Remember that in the time of Darwin, the world was (and still is) completely entranced by the wonders of religion. At the time, the most accepted theories on the origins of the universe and of human civilization as we know it stemmed from religious origin stories, mythical lore and folktales.

However, Darwin, and many other freethinkers of the world, theorized that there was something more to it. Human beings didn't just appear out of thin air. According to Darwin, it wasn't as if one day, there were no people in the world and then the next day they just willed themselves into existence. Nope. Darwin introduced the Theory of Evolution by Natural Selection. This scientific theory would later go on to revolutionize the way people thought about existence and their place in the universe.

In Darwin's theory, he proposed that human beings are merely byproducts of numerous evolutionary processes that span over a very long period of time. He attributes the formidable existence of human civilization to the ability of the species to adapt to its environment. To put it simply, Darwin believed that we are all here today because we were able to understand what it took to survive in the world that we live in. This is where the old adage, *survival of the fittest*, stems from.

Throughout the course of history, mankind has been responsible for a myriad of amazing milestones and accomplishments. As a species, we developed technologies that enabled us to shoot up into the sky and into space. We created great pieces of art that evoked strong bursts of emotion. We invented amazing devices that allowed us to instantly communicate with another human in another part of the world. The human species has really had a rich and interesting history. However, it hasn't always been a good one.

Every now and then, a certain threat emerges that seeks to unravel the very thread that our species has slowly been building over millennia. Sometimes, these threats are man-made. World wars and geopolitical disputes are constantly threatening the fabric of society. Global warming is a continuous threat that is slowly killing off numerous species in the world. But there's one particular threat that has proven to be just as deadly as any of those that we've mentioned so far: pandemics.

# A History of Pandemics

Human beings have managed to spread out all around the world. And since there are human beings on just about every place on earth, infectious diseases are ever present as well. Sure, throughout the course of human history we have managed to yield major advancements in the fields of medical practice and technology. Our medical treatment these days is more sophisticated than ever. We have the best tools and the best doctors in the history of our species. However, in spite of this, outbreaks of disease are continuous mainstays in modern society. Some diseases don't really make much of a dent in the grander scheme of things. However, there are certain illnesses that really demand to be paid attention to and are classified as more advanced forms of disease due to their global reach and severity. Often, these illnesses are referred to as pandemics.

Should human beings really fear pandemics? Well, as history tells us, we have a pretty good track record when it comes to preserving our species in the face of massive outbreaks of disease. So, if you're looking for a short answer, "no." Human beings are probably going to continue to survive pandemics for a very long time and we probably shouldn't fear extinction (due to a pandemic, at least). However, that isn't to say that we should underestimate these disease-causing bacteria and viruses. Yes, we may be evolving as a species, but they are evolving as well. In any pandemic, there are bound to be casualties. This is why you still need to understand that you have certain roles and responsibilities that you need to play to minimize the onslaught that these pandemics may bring.

Examples of pandemics have been around for all of humankind. In relatively recent history, during the period of 1918 to 1919, the biggest pandemic to ever threaten human civilization took the lives of around 50 million people. In that entire year, more than 500 million people were infected with the disease. This was the Spanish Flu pandemic, a disease that was brought about by an H1N1 virus from pigs. The pandemic was so serious that it even pushed certain indigenous groups towards extinction. At the time, World War I was in full force. This only exasperated the problem as soldiers were exposed to extremely unhealthy living conditions, day in and day out. Despite its name, the Spanish Flu didn't actually originate in Spain. It just so happened that Spain wasn't an active participant in the war and had healthy journalistic practices. As such, their press was free to report on the outbreak of the illness in various military camps while other nations sought to suppress it.

In more recent history, the Swine Flu, which originated in 2009, has already infected more than 100 million Americans. It was dubbed by many as a "silent killer" as not a lot of people had really developed much awareness of the disease, and very little government control was imposed in suppressing it. However, the disease has managed to take the lives of more than 75,000 people since it first burst onto the scene.

The last outbreak of early 2020 wasn't the first pandemic in recent human history. It's also not the most prominent one in terms of number of infected patients and death tolls. It's also not going to be the last pandemic we ever see. However, as we continue to face our ever-changing world, we need to consciously remind ourselves that the next big pandemic is coming. And we have to know what to do to prepare for it when it comes.

# Fighting for Survival in the Present and Future

In spite of the many pandemics that we have conquered as a species, the Darwinian principles still ring true today. There is no room for complacency. You do not have the luxury of staying comfortable for too long. As human beings, we get more and more advanced as each day goes by. However, our threats become more complicated and more advanced as well. This is why we must always make it a point to know what we can do to protect ourselves and all of those that we love.

Self-preservation isn't something to be ashamed about. It's an innate aspect of what makes us human. It's also what is responsible for our species persisting as long as it has. Hopefully, it will continue to be responsible for allowing us to carry on towards the future. Again, those who fail to adapt will fail to survive. This is precisely why it's absolutely integral that we never stop fighting for our survival. We must never give up on principles of self-preservation. Our natural instinct as human beings is to always fight for our survival. It's something primal and it's embedded into the core of our very nature.

This book is a manifestation of that nature; a contribution to the causes of self-preservation. In order for you to adapt to the world that you are living in, it's important that you are able to understand its many nuances to the best of your abilities. This includes you taking the time to understand the many threats that you continually face every day. And the threat that we will be focusing on in the chapters to come will be pandemics, and how to get through them safely.

As you make your way through this book, you should be able to develop and gain more profound insights into pandemics and how they fit into our society. More than that, you should also be able to develop a better understanding of your inherent duties to make sure that you keep yourself protected in times of mass outbreaks. Also, you must take the time to learn about the role that you need to play in your community in fighting these diseases. Make no mistake about it. A pandemic is a disease that threatens the lives of potentially millions of people all around the world. And in most cases, it's going to take a communal effort to fight off these diseases.

Dealing with pandemics is no laughing matter. It's also not an easy feat. It's a very complicated process that is vastly dependent on the mass cooperation of well-informed individuals who understand the responsibilities that they need to live up to. You don't have to be a medical professional or a world leader to participate and contribute to fighting a pandemic. In fact, I'll argue that if you're a member of the masses, then you have the biggest responsibility of all. Mobilization is key when it comes to dealing with pandemics. And with mass mobilizations, knowledge sharing and information gathering are tantamount.

This is why it's a good sign that you're reading materials like this. It's proof that your self-preservation instincts are kicking in. It means that you do have an innate desire for survival and you're willing to do all that is necessary for you to make it in this world. Hopefully, this book will be able to contribute to your desires to adapt yourself to the conditions set forth by this ever-changing world.

As they say, you can never really control everything that happens to you in life. There are just some things that happen in the world which are beyond your control or scope of influence. However, what you can do is choose how you react to certain conditions. You can always decide on how you would respond to certain challenges. No one ever really designs pandemics to emerge or propagate the way that they do. It's something that just happens and is beyond the control of most people in the world. But that doesn't mean that people should just give up altogether and give in to the disease. You still have the power to decide how you will respond to these threats.

Hopefully, by reading this book, you will be placed in a much better position to respond to threats of disease in a more responsible and wholesome manner. When Darwin was first talking about the survival of the fittest idea, it was likely that he had the hunter-gatherer ecosystem in mind. Only the fittest human beings who were capable of hunting and gathering for their food were able to survive. In the earliest days of human civilization, physical fitness was important. However, mental acuity is also just as essential to one's survival. Reading books like these will add to your breadth of knowledge, hereby making you more equipped to face the many threats and challenges of your environment. So, here's to expanding your knowledge. Here's to your survival.

21

**CHAPTER 1:**

# Social Distancing

In this modern age, whenever pandemics arise, one of the most common and powerful tools that human beings can use to combat disease is to engage in social distancing. Of course, social distancing is really more of just a colloquial phrase that people attribute to the act of physically establishing distance between one individual from another. It also comes in a variety of different names such as self-quarantining or flattening the curve. While they may differ by labels, the principles of such methods are all essentially the same. They are all trying to impose physical isolation from other people in an effort to lessen the effectiveness of the virus.

Okay, that all might seem a little ridiculous or vague to you at the moment. But there is a real science behind social distancing. There's a reason why organizations like the WHO and the CDC all advocate the idea of social distancing when trying to control outbreaks of highly contagious diseases. This chapter is going to discuss everything that you might need to know about social distancing.

How does it work? Why is it effective? Who has to do social distancing? How long will social distancing be in effect? These are all questions that we are going to try to answer as we make our way deeper into this chapter.

At its core, it's really easy to denounce social distancing because of the many implications that the implementation of such a measure would bring. In its most modest form, an imposition of social distancing would mean people not being able to go to mass gatherings like parties, concerts, and other such events.

But in its most extreme forms, social distancing might also entail the total shutdown of various establishments and industries to make sure that people stay at home. There are varying degrees and forms of social distancing. I think it's critically important to understand the principles behind it in order to really grasp why this tool can be mankind's best bet in fighting against diseases and outbreaks of deadly viruses.

## What Is Social Distancing?

Social distancing means that you're not going to get a chance to go to the basketball game that you've already paid tickets for. It means that you won't get to push through with that wedding even when you've already made all of the reservations and bookings months prior. It means that you're not going to get to go on that flight to Europe that you've been saving up for for so long. Sure, if that's what your first encounter with the idea of social distancing is going to be, it's understandable that you wouldn't like it. However, what you just have to keep in mind in spite of your dislike of the situation, social distancing can dramatically help slow down or even potentially stop the spread of the disease.

What social distancing really means is that human beings make a conscious effort to distance themselves from one another. In its mildest forms, social distancing can be done in an informal manner wherein people just avoid social situations altogether. However, whenever outbreaks of disease get too serious, it's possible that social distancing becomes an institutionalized matter. In the most extreme cases, institutionalized social distancing means the temporary closure or suspension of operations for various establishments (both public and private). This might mean that you won't get the chance to go to the office the way that you typically could for your work. Maybe, you won't get to visit your favorite malls, restaurants, or bars anymore to engage in your usual activities.

To make it simple, social distancing is just merely establishing physical space between yourself and another person. Some organizations recommend that you maintain a distance as far as six feet in order to perform social distancing properly. As human beings, we have evolved to become a society that promotes interacting in close proximities. However, with social distancing, you have to do away with those notions. When you're engaged in social distancing, it could potentially mean:

- working from home instead of going to the office
- closing down schools and having students use e-learning portals instead

- communicating with others only through digital media
- postponing, rescheduling, or just downright cancelling big events like conferences, meetings, weddings, parties, etc.

Social distancing is a genuine disruption of the way that you would typically conduct yourself in everyday life. It's not just going to alter the manner in which you interact with other people; it's also going to dramatically alter the way that the entire society functions. All sorts of corporate, political, and social institutions are going to have to fundamentally change the way that they function when social distancing is enforced to its greatest degrees.

## *Who is Social Distancing For?*

In order to isolate the disease, it's important that everyone partake in social distancing. To put it simply, social distancing, if it's going to work, is something that everyone has to actively participate in. Of course, the levels of practicing social distancing will differ from person to person. There are some individuals who are essential to keeping society afloat in times of a pandemic. Examples of such individuals include essential government workers, community leaders, medical professionals, sanitary or janitorial professionals, food and beverage suppliers, medical equipment manufacturers, and so on.

But when we're talking about the general public as a whole, everyone has to actively participate in social distancing. This also includes basic sanitary habits that will keep you and your loved ones safer during a pandemic. Some basic tenets of social distancing includes:

- practice good sanitation and cleansing habits

- avoid sharing items like utensils, towels, and even beds (if one person is sick, especially)
- stay at home and don't entertain visitors
- only leave the house for essential errands like grocery shopping
- when out in public, maintain a distance of six feet from other people
- avoid handshakes, hugs, kisses, and other forms of physical contact

Again, social distancing is a total upheaval of the way that we typically live our lives. But is such a dramatic measure necessary? Will it even work?

# How Does Social Distancing Work?

Now, you might already have a good understanding of what social distancing is and how to practice it. However, you might not still have the faintest idea of how it works and why it would be an effective measure against fighting disease. Well, the truth is that social distancing is a measure that proves its effectiveness in different ways. In general, its primary purpose is to serve as a tool to fight against an outbreak or a pandemic. However, this can still be broken down into more specific outputs that are less abstract and more tangible.

### *It Protects You from Getting Infected or from Infecting Others*

Of course, the first obvious byproduct of social distancing is that it prevents you from getting infected by other people with the disease and vice-versa. If you are physically well, and then you shut yourself in and isolate yourself from others, you are giving yourself the best form of protection against the virus. Usually, disease-causing bacteria and germs can only be spread through human beings when multiple individuals come into contact with one another. So, when you engage in social distancing, you are dramatically minimizing the chances of you contracting the disease.

However, there is another level to this as well. There are certain people who might be asymptomatic in times of a pandemic. What this means is that they might be infected with the disease, but not realize it because they aren't exhibiting symptoms. It's scary when you're asymptomatic because you might be unknowingly spreading the disease to people you interact with. You may not have symptoms, and they might not necessarily have as strong an immune system as you do. So, when you partake in social distancing and you quarantine yourself, you minimize the chances of you giving the disease off to someone else. You are protecting others who are vulnerable, which is the very basis of a participatory society.

### *It Flattens the Curve*

Another phrase that you might hear a lot during a pandemic is the idea of flattening the curve. The curve that people are talking about here is the one that you would find on a graph depicting the rates of infection in a population over a certain period of time. The more people get infected within a short period, then the more pronounced the curve is going to look like on that graph. What people mean when they say that they want to flatten the curve is that they want to spread the rates of infection over a more extended period of time. When people aren't getting infected over a prolonged period, the curve will drop and will continue to do so until it resembles a line or a flattened state.

The reason that flattening the curve is critically important in an epidemic is that it protects the capacity of the healthcare system. Usually, outbreaks occur and become aggravated when too many people are getting sick and the demand for treatment surpasses the capable supply. To put it simply, when too many people are sick at the same time, it paralyzes hospitals, pharmaceutical companies, doctors, nurses, and other stakeholders in the healthcare system. When this happens, it means that healthcare staff who need personal protective equipment (PPE) like face masks and gloves won't have access to important gear. It can also mean that patients who need a respirator will not receive the treatment that they need and may succumb to the disease, unnecessarily. However, when society is able to flatten the curve and spread the rate of infection out over a prolonged period, then the healthcare industry will be better equipped to provide proper treatment to the people who have become ill.

### It Helps Kill or Stop the Spread of the Virus

Lastly, social distancing can potentially help slow down or even stop the spread of the virus altogether. You see, viruses need hosts in order for them to survive. This is why pandemics are always a virus's best-case scenario. When society isn't practicing sensible outbreak protocols, the attacking virus is able to jump from one host to another and perpetuate. As they continue to multiply, they are able to amass more strength. However, when proper social distancing protocols are put in place and are properly executed by the masses, viruses will slowly dwindle out until they become extinct. Without a host to latch onto, a virus won't be able to survive for too long.

## Some Problems with Social Distancing

There, now you have a better idea of how social distancing can help minimize the harmful effects of a pandemic. In fact, it might be the best solution to overcoming pandemics altogether. However, that doesn't mean that it doesn't come without its caveats and problems. There are still plenty of drawbacks to a full implementation of a social distancing protocol. In the interest of fairness, here are a few caveats and disadvantages that come with the mass implementation of social distancing:

## Harmful for Some Peoples' Mental Health

There are just certain people who need to interact with others in order for them to remain sane. Obviously, with social distancing, physical interactions are severely limited. This can be damaging with people who are struggling with mental issues and who rely on the physical interactions that they share with the other people in their lives. On top of that, social distancing and self-quarantining can be a very traumatic and stressful ordeal for a lot of people. All of this added stress brought about by panic and uncertainty could further damage the already delicate psyche for someone who is battling with mental health issues.

## *Cancellation of Important Events and Gatherings*

When social distancing is institutionalized, this typically means that mass gatherings of any sort are discouraged or just downright cancelled. This means that weddings that are prepared, planned and paid for, often many months in advance, need to be put on hold. International conferences and seminars that involve intricate logistical efforts will have to be delayed for now. Concerts, sporting events, movie premieres and other such recreational gatherings will also have to be put on hold.

### *Damaging to the Economy*

And lastly, there is the inevitable damage that social distancing is going to cause the economy. On one level, you have the various establishments and businesses that rely on foot traffic for them to survive. Without people going out and venturing into stores to buy products and services, there is no cash flow. And if this goes on for a long enough period of time, it could potentially force a lot of small businesses and their owners and/or employees to go through extremely difficult times, including bankruptcy.

Also, there is the issue of the laborers and workers as well. For some of the privileged few, their income doesn't necessarily have to stop as they can still provide productive work from within the confines of their homes. However, there are many laborers and workers who don't have the sweet luxury of working from home.

Thus, their inability to go to work and earn a living leaves them without any income for an indefinite amount of time.

A prolonged community quarantine could do irreversible damage to the economic situations of many places, especially those within developing nations, or those who are economically disadvantaged, even in the wealthiest of countries or cities.

## Final Thoughts

Social distancing might not be a luxury that is going to be welcomed by most people in the world. In fact, a vast majority of us thrive when we can venture out into the world and interact with other people. It's what, in the very least, defines a typical society - social engagement. However, as the cliche goes, desperate times call for desperate measures. And don't doubt the fact that a pandemic is definitely a time for desperation. While the measures to counteract the spread of a virus might seem a little extreme to most people, they really are necessary most of the time.

But in order for any measure to be carried out and practiced in an effective and meaningful manner, people need to really understand the principles behind such measures. Through a developed understanding of social distancing, it's more likely that people will truly adopt these precautionary measures properly so as to limit the spread and strength of a virus.

**CHAPTER 2:**

# How Will We Live in a Pandemic State?

Now, on to matters of living in a pandemic state. Obviously, the way that you would live your life in the middle of a pandemic is not necessarily natural, nor is it ideal. In fact, it might be a completely alien concept to you and it's going to require a lot of adjustments on your part. You are going to have to make certain changes to the way that you structure your everyday life. Again, it's going to differ on a case to case basis. For instance, the typical everyday routine for a doctor fighting on the frontlines of the pandemic is going to be different from an entrepreneur who now has to resort to working at home.

We've already touched upon the principles of social distancing. We've talked about how this is a necessary tactic in flattening the curve and preventing the spread of the virus. You have also been briefed on some of the major disadvantages and caveats that come with the institutionalization of social distancing policies. However, you might still not really have a good idea of what it means to be living in a pandemic state. Sure, you have all of the generalities covered, but you might still be unsure of what your day-to-day life is going to look like.

This segment of the book will try to give you a clearer glimpse into the way that the world is going to function when there's a pandemic. The way that a community functions when it's under a pandemic state is going to be fundamentally different for a lot of different sectors. Again, it's not going to be the most natural way to live life. There is going to be a standard level of flexibility that will be required of all of us.

In order to navigate the uncertainties and chaos that comes with dealing with a pandemic, this chapter is going to offer up some valuable insights and potential solutions. If you are someone who might struggle with adjusting to living a life of social distancing, lockdowns, and community quarantines, don't be afraid. You're not alone. Everyone is going through all of the same struggles as you are. Everyone is also trying to figure things out as they go. But if you're really in need of some guidance, then I think this chapter will help you feel more comfortable and prepared.

# Stay Productive

The very first thing that you have to keep in mind when you're living in a pandemic is that you have to still stay productive. Yes, to a certain extent, the virus is continually crippling the world and limiting its mobility. However, that shouldn't mean that it's okay for you to be completely unproductive throughout the course of a pandemic. Fortunately, these days, technology has afforded us the capacity to still be productive without even having to step one foot outside of the house. You can practically conquer the whole world from the confines of your bedroom if you want to. Modern technology allows us to do this. Let's delve into this a little bit more.

## *Try to Work*

This is a tip that is going to be expounded further upon in the next chapter of this book. Although, to put it simply, wherever you can, try to do some work. If you have a job that allows for you to work from home, then you should do so. Remind yourself that you still have to earn a living in order to sustain yourself. Also, there are lots of people all over the world who have jobs that can't be performed from home. So, when you have that opportunity to do so, capitalize on it. Working is also a healthy distraction, as when you're working, you're not stressing about the pandemic.

## *Learn New Skills*

You may end up having a lot of extra time if you're going to be staying at home all day. Even if you're working at home, often you still have more time since you don't have to get ready for work, or commute to/from your job. Try to make the most out of that time to learn new skills or to practice old ones. For instance, you might have been putting off learning how to play a guitar that you bought a few months back. Now is the perfect time for you to take that hobby up again. Maybe you could try learning new recipes and try some new techniques in your kitchen. Whatever the case, it's important that you find a way to still adopt a learner's mindset. This way, you are constantly growing even though you're stuck at home. Like working, this is also a positive distraction from stressful news about the pandemic.

### *Catch Up on Books, Shows, Movies*

Relax and engage in a few forms of recreation for a bit. Again, you're likely to have extra time on your hands. If you have always been grappling with a busy schedule in your typical lifestyle, then a self-imposed quarantine would be a great time for you to relax a little bit. Read some of the books that have been sitting idle on your bookshelf. Watch those television shows and movies that you've been meaning to see for the longest time now. Browse and scour the internet for various forms of media to keep you entertained. In this day and age, there is definitely no shortage of media.

### *Exercise*

This is one thing that you really have to make a point to do even when you're practicing social distancing. If your area allows it, try going for a run or even just a long walk. Just make sure that you're maintaining a solid distance of at least 6 feet from other people you might encounter along the way. If you're not leaving your house, then try doing home workouts instead. There are loads of different home-safe workouts and exercise routines that you can get into just to keep yourself in shape. Remember, in times of a pandemic, it's important that you really boost your immune system. And part of doing so means exercising regularly.

## Stay Updated

Next, you have a responsibility to stay updated. In a time of a pandemic, there are many developments that are taking place, both good and bad. It's very important that you make it a point to stay updated on these developments so that you are always aware of any vital information that you might need to survive. Of course, pandemics are scary. And one of the scariest aspects of the pandemic is all of the uncertainty that surrounds it. This is why information gathering is absolutely vital. You have to make it a point to really find out more about what's happening around you so that you are better equipped to deal with the pandemic.

### Read Content from Trusted Media Outlets

In times of a pandemic, you have to be very wary of the information that you source and gather. Currently, in the age of mass information, there is an inordinate amount of fake news that is circulating around the internet.

Be sure that you are only reading news from reputable sources so that you won't be victimized by alternative facts. To be sure about it, be sure to subscribe to any newsletters or updates from the CDC (Center for Disease Control) or the WHO (World Health Organization). Also, subscribe to updates from your local media outlets.

## *Share Information Yourself*

Next, you also might want to consider being a bastion for information sharing as well. If you have any dedicated channels or messaging platforms for news updates on the pandemic, feel free to share whatever news you are able to gather. One of the best parts about the internet is the freedom to spread vital information in the blink of an eye. So, do not minimize whatever impact you might have. You have your own social network and they might be able to benefit from whatever news that you have to share. But again, remind yourself to only share news from reputable sources.

You don't want to be that person who causes panic or induces toxic positivity with fake news stories that are only perpetuating political agendas or designed to cause uncertainty and distrust in society.

## Stay Stocked Up

Ideally, you will want to limit going out as much as possible when you're in the middle of a lockdown. So, whenever you do decide to run to the grocery, you want to make sure that you're really stocking up for the long haul when it comes to your general necessities and supplies. Granted, the needs of every household are going to be vastly different. A bachelor living in a studio apartment isn't going to need as many supplies as a family who lives in a 4-bedroom household. There's no need to hoard - calculate what you will need for 3-4 weeks of staying at home, and purchase that, plus maybe 25 percent more, just in case.

There are some universal necessities that EVERYONE needs to stock up on during a period of lockdown. It's merely a matter of adjusting on quantity to accommodate the number of people living in a single household. Here are a few of those necessities:

food with long shelf-life:

canned fish

rice, oats, or pasta (as opposed to bread which spoils quickly)

beans and legumes

nuts

nut butters

dried fruit

canned vegetables

canned meats

coffee

pet food (for your pets)

water, etc.

general toiletries:

soaps (hand soap, body soap, facial washes)

shampoos

toothpaste

toothbrushes

mouthwash

shaving cream

razors

hand sanitizers

moisturizers

astringents, etc.

general household supplies:

toilet paper

table napkins

dishwashing liquid

laundry detergent

floor cleaners, etc.

medicine and multivitamins

## Stay Social

Lastly, you still want to make it a point to stay social. Keep in mind that social distancing only ever really refers to physical distancing. Just because you are stuck in a pandemic doesn't have to mean that you should be totally isolating yourself from the rest of the world. In fact, in times of crises, it's very important that people band together and still espouse a sense of community.

Again, fortunately for us, we can always choose to avail of the powers of the internet. You still have the capacity to interact with the people who are also living in your household. This is a great opportunity for families to really bond and build the ties that they have together. Also, feel free to reach out to your friends and loved ones via digital platforms. Find out how they're doing and try to stay updated on how their lives are going.

This is going to help build a sense of camaraderie within society and that's always healthy. This is especially going to be beneficial for people who really crave social interactions. It can be incredibly therapeutic to just have a conversation with a dear friend or someone you care about. You might even forget about all the stress that you're experiencing during such trying times.

# Find Out How You Can Help

Of course, you have to recognize that you are still a member of the larger community. You not only have a responsibility to yourself, but also to the people around you. Pandemics are hard on a lot of people. However, they are definitely going to be much more difficult for the marginalized and the less fortunate. So, if you are a person of privilege, try to make an effort to find out how you can be of help to the people around you. Assistance and charity in a time of crises is not compulsory. You always have to make it a point to prioritize your own needs and those of your loved ones. However, wherever you can be of assistance to people who badly need it, try to live up to that. Even a few dollars or cans of food can really help someone.

# Practice Responsible Social Distancing

Lastly, we have to go back to responsible social distancing. It's very important to stress the importance of this practice to make sure that the virus slows down and a pandemic is weakened. While it can be incredibly frustrating to have to bear with life under the principles of social distancing, it's absolutely necessary. And the stricter you are with the implementation of it, the sooner we will be able to kill the virus dead in its tracks. We've already exhausted all talks of social distancing in the previous chapter. This is just a reminder that you need to incorporate social distancing principles in the way that you structure your life in the middle of a pandemic.

# Final Thoughts

It's definitely a big adjustment and no one is understating how difficult this is going to be for a lot of people. But a pandemic can change the world in very significant ways. A failure to adjust and adapt to the call of the times could lead to catastrophic results. This is why it's very important to implement all of the best practices with regards to living life in a pandemic state. Obviously, it's not going to be easy for anyone. However, human civilization has proven its resilience time and time again.

All that this chapter was able to provide you was a deeper glimpse into what a life in a pandemic state might look like. However, things can still get a lot more complicated than that depending on where you live or what kind of lifestyle you have. Hopefully, this chapter will have provided you with all of the necessary building blocks that you need to craft a pandemic-friendly lifestyle as you wait for the crisis to subside. Again, no one should ever expect the process to be an easy one. In fact, you should expect it to be the total opposite. But this is not a crisis that is totally impossible to overcome. One should always remind themselves of the fact that better days are coming and that there is life after a pandemic.

**CHAPTER 3:**

# The Shut-In Economy

Just because a pandemic is going on doesn't mean that the economy has to stop in its tracks. In fact, the world's economy should still find a way to keep on pushing on to the best of its abilities in spite of the pandemic. However, that's a lot harder than it sounds. Obviously, when there are all sorts of social distancing policies that are in place; it can be very hard for businesses to function properly. If you own a restaurant, you're obviously not getting the same kind of foot traffic that you're used to. If you own a clothing store, you aren't getting customers to come into your boutique to fit clothes anymore. If you're a cab driver, you're obviously not going to be able to drive people around because no one is going anywhere.

A lot of people are physically suffering as a result of being infected by this disease. However, in times of a pandemic, even those who are healthy and immune from the disease are still impacted significantly. Everyone in the world is affected by a pandemic in one way or another. And one of the most significant ways that people are affected in a major pandemic is that they can lose their source of income. Of course, it's very different if you have emergency savings to fall back on. But not everyone is going to last for so long without any cash coming in. Most of us don't have substantial savings, anyway, since we scrape by - paycheck by paycheck.

The economics of a pandemic are always going to be very complicated. But it's still important that community leaders still try their best to keep the economy afloat during such stressful and tense times. The world shouldn't be forced to shut down altogether just because there's a pandemic going on. Keeping the economy afloat is also a way of fighting back against the pandemic. However, given the sensitivity of the situation, there are indeed a few proper ways to go about doing so.

This chapter is going to help walk you through a few simple principles and tips that you could apply to your personal situation. Granted, not everyone is going to have the same kind of economic setup. This is why policy enactment and enforcement in a time like this is just too tricky. There are too many industries and types of businesses that need to be taken into consideration. So, for now, it would be best for us, as individuals, to just do you part by looking out for ourselves, and others, as much as we can. Regardless if you're the owner of a struggling start-up or if you're an employee in a big conglomerate, there are some very specific things that you can do to make sure that the economy keeps rolling on.

While this chapter is going to try to be as comprehensive and exhaustive as possible, again, there is still a good chance that not all of its contents will be applicable to your life. When that is the case, you still have to do your part in being inventive. Allow your primal nature to take over and fight for your survival.

## Working from Home

Staying at home is not an excuse for you to be inactive and unproductive. Depending on the nature of your work, it's still very much possible for you to work from home. It's just a matter of you finding a systematic way of going about things. Like it is in any professional environment, there are a few best practices that you can employ to make sure that you're still at your best. Of course, it's going to be a different system for business owners and those who are employees or workers. Try to follow the tips listed here so that you are still putting yourself in the best position to be productive. While the circumstances are dramatically different, you still have the capacity to produce substantial output with your work.

## *Working from Home for Business Owners and Entrepreneurs*

If you are a business owner, then it's likely that you are the leader of your organization. Even if you're top-level or middle-level management, you still have a significant scope of influence and power over the people that you're working with. This is why there is a lot of responsibility that falls on your plate in a time of crisis. It's your job to steer the ship in the middle of a storm. So, if you don't know what to do, don't worry. Just remember a few of these key things:

1. Review pending projects and deliverables - It's possible that before you went into quarantine, there were a bunch of projects that you had yet to accomplish. If that's the case, you have to make it a point to finish them even while you're on quarantine. Generate a rundown of pending deliverables so that you are aware of the things that you need to get done.

2. Mobilize the team - In the advent of technology, it's so much easier for people to work and collaborate as a team in spite of distance. Working remotely might be a challenge, but it's not an impossible feat altogether. Make use of various software tools and apps to make team coordination and communication more efficient and effective. Online platforms like Slack, Zoom, Skype and other virtual office and meeting spaces

can keep you and your business on track.

3. Seek out new projects or clients - Just because you're on lockdown doesn't mean that you shouldn't be looking for new business. Try communicating with people in your network and see if you can offer your services or products. If you're staying active with your entrepreneurial pursuits, it's just as likely that other people are doing the same.

***Working from Home for Regular Employees and Workers***

Working from home is different when you're a regular employee or staff member. If you don't have a managerial position that includes a leadership and supervisory role, it can be hard to stay motivated when working at home. Since you'll be much more independent, and not under the watchful eyes of your supervisor, and your colleagues, staying focused and on-task can be a real struggle. Here are a few things that you can try out to make yourself more productive and focused.

1. Communicate with leaders and managers regularly - The best practice would be for you to deliver daily EOD's or end of day reports. This way, your immediate superior is always aware of what's on your plate. When they know that you're busy with projects, they won't overload you. If they see that you have a rather empty plate, they can give you more responsibility.

2. Dress like you mean it - Sure, it can be really tempting to just lounge around in your pajamas all day while you're on lockdown. However, it really helps to dress the part. Putting on your work clothes before you get started on your work will put you in the right mindset.

Even if you don't put on your formal work clothes, it's important to shower, stay groomed, and change your clothes from home-time, to work-time.

3. Manage your finances properly - Obviously, if you are an employee or a worker, then you rely on your regular paycheck to sustain yourself. Given that the pandemic is putting a lot of businesses on hazardous grounds, you should try to find alternate sources of income that you can control on your own. Fortunately, with the internet, there are many ways in which you can monetize your skills without having to leave your room.

# Managing Your Finances

Money management in a time of crisis is very important. When big pandemics hit, it's very likely that the world's economy will be seriously affected, and perhaps experience catastrophic damage. This is why, as an individual, you have to do your part in making sure that you are safe and secure until things stabilize again. And that might take a while. So, if you aren't someone who has an enormous bank account to keep you tied over, then you might want to consider really taking note of the way that you're managing your money. You would never want to end up in a state of poverty under any circumstance, but especially when there's a pandemic going on. While there are all sorts of resources out there that you can exhaust for money management, here are a few general reminders that you might want to keep to heart.

## *Budgeting for the Long Haul*

Make sure that you're budgeting your money for the long haul. Sure, some governments might place proper schedules and time limits for lockdowns or quarantine periods. However, you can't take all of those policies at face value. There is a chance that situations might become complicated and the lockdowns may be enforced for longer periods than initially anticipated. This is why you really want to take a worst-case scenario approach to budgeting here. Try calculating how much money you're still able to bring in and compute how much money you're spending every month. Dedicate a certain amount of your income to emergency savings that you won't touch until there's an actual emergency. Whatever money is left over from your income is the cash that you should allot for expenses and savings. If you aren't saving enough cash, then you might have to make sacrifices to limit your spending.

## *Making Smart Investments*

In a pandemic state, think of every purchase that you make as a necessary investment. So, if you buy food or pay for utilities, think of these things as investments for your survival. Naturally, you wouldn't want to invest in anything that is not considered essential to your survival. This means that you should look to hold off on any excessive or unnecessary shopping for the meantime. If you have some extra cash left over from savings, then maybe you can look into long-term investments like stocks and bonds.

## *Maximizing Government Welfare and Support*

If you're lucky enough to have a government that is offering welfare and support for its citizens, then you need to maximize that. Try to make sure that you are updated and aware of any government efforts to subsidize the struggles of its citizens. Depending on where you live, governments might offer subsidies in the forms of cash or relief goods. Whatever the case, you shouldn't be too proud to accept these forms of support or welfare. During a time of crises, any single asset counts. So, whatever opportunity you can get your hands on, it's important that you maximize it.

## Find New Skills or New Income Streams

Unfortunately, not everyone is going to have the luxury of converting their typical work life into a situation wherein you can still work from home. For example, car technicians might not be able to earn much of a living when staying at home. So, given that, it's important that some people really take the time during quarantine to learn new skills and find new income streams. This might be a lot easier said than done, but it's important to be able to adapt to the times if you are to survive.

Unfortunately, the pandemic isn't going to take pity on you just because you lost a source of income. You have to be able to fend for yourself.

If you're completely lost on this, check into some of the online job/gig platforms like Upwork, Fiverr, Guru, and FlexJobs. Through these platforms, you can highlight whatever skills you have to connect with potential clients. Granted, you might need to develop certain skill sets to be competitive in the online job space, but it's never too late to develop new skills anyway. This is especially true when you're in lockdown and you have more time to study and practice. Additionally, the competition for jobs or gigs is stiff - so make sure you put together a nice profile and portfolio, and expect to take lower paying tasks to build up your references and reviews.

# Supporting Your Local Economy

Again, very few businesses are going to be immune from the treacheries and damages brought about by a pandemic. Unless you run a huge corporation that has been established for many years, you might not have the kind of financial security you wish you could have in times like these. It's also the same for all of the small businesses that are within your local economy. So, barbershops, bakeries, carwashes, farmer's markets, butcher shops, and others might struggle greatly when there's a pandemic. So, whenever you can, try to make an effort to support small and local businesses. Rather than buying a loaf of bread from a corporation, try buying from a local bakery instead. It's little adjustments like these that can really make a difference in the lives of so many entrepreneurs and small businesses.

# Final Thoughts

On the surface, a pandemic is a genuine health crisis. There's a deadly disease that's roaming around out there just waiting to infect whatever host it can manage to land. However, to a certain extent, it's also a political crisis. Leaders and politicians all over the world are looking to enforce laws and policies to make sure that a pandemic is managed properly and that damages are mitigated as much as possible. However, on top of all of that, a pandemic is also an economic crisis. When people are immobilized and are disallowed from partaking in their usual everyday routines, it can really disrupt the way money moves around.

Pandemics are already inherently tricky events to have to overcome. There are so many layers attached to a health crisis and so many efforts need to be undertaken to suppress an outbreak. But there are so many other added layers that need to be addressed as well. By focusing our money on the local economy, and through careful financial planning, you and your neighbors can come out of this crisis unscathed, or at least in a position where financial devastation is not permanent.

**CHAPTER 4:**

# Social Life Repercussions

We've already talked about how a pandemic is primarily a health issue. Obviously, when the threat of a powerful virus emerges, it's important that health experts and medical professionals come together to lead us towards a place of safety and protection. More than anything else, the pandemic is a health issue. However, we also talked about how pandemics are also economic issues. When a pandemic forces people into self-imposed quarantines and lockdowns, economies will suffer. Our modern society is designed for people to always be moving around and staying mobile. However, the presence of a pandemic might render the luxury of mobility completely void. So, in that sense, it's very much likely that the lack of human mobility will create a huge dent in economic systems all over the world. And no one will be spared from this, whether rich or poor. Clearly, however, the socially and economically disadvantaged will have a much more difficult time.

But there is another layer to a pandemic that we haven't talked about yet. Pandemics are also social issues. Keep in mind that a pandemic is a crisis. Usually, in times of crises, there is a tendency for mass hysteria and panic to take place. Human beings aren't always going to have the most rational reactions to a crisis. In fact, it might even be safe to assume that a society could potentially devolve into complete chaos when faced with a brutal threat like a pandemic. These irrational or erratic behaviors might be significant enough to actually create a dent in the social fabric of society.

What this chapter is going to look into is how the social lives of people are going to play out when faced with a pandemic. We already briefly touched on some of these concepts earlier. Weddings might have to be cancelled. Sporting events might have to be put on hold. Movie premiers will have to be rescheduled to later dates. As trivial as these events might seem, they are still integral aspects of the social experience. And when it gets to a point wherein the social fabric of society becomes dramatically compromised, it can lead to some very weird and potentially undesirable outcomes.

In this chapter, I will try to help you manage your expectations so that you will be in a better position to deal with the social fallouts of a pandemic. Again, you are going to have to make some very big adjustments when you're going to overcome a pandemic. Life is going to be turned on its head. This means that you're going to have to readjust the way that you interact with other people, whether it be physically or not. Part of being able to overcome a pandemic in a quicker and more rapid pace is if human beings do it together. However, that sense of togetherness might be lost as a result of certain social fallouts.

This is why it's important for you to still understand your role as a person in your community and your social circle. These days, we are more connected than we have ever been because of the internet. It's so easy for a person from another part of the globe who doesn't even know you exist to read about something that you post on your social media platforms. Given that, you have to take it upon yourself to be a more socially responsible individual, especially in a time of crisis.

# Dealing with Mass Social Gatherings

Human interaction is a very basic and integral aspect of life. As the old cliché goes, no man is an island. We try our best to always be independent and self-sufficient. However, at the end of the day, we rely on the companionship and support of the people around us in order to really maximize our individual potential. The problem with the persistence of a pandemic is that it forces people to isolate themselves from one another. When typically, mass gatherings are a natural occurrence in everyday life, this is something that is greatly discouraged in a time of a pandemic. So, it's no secret that social distancing is dramatically impacting the way that people conduct their social lives.

## *Dealing with Public Celebrations Like Weddings or Birthdays*

Expect to experience any major life milestones or celebrations on your own. Typically, when there is a cause for celebration, people gather together and celebrate as a single community. However, this is a luxury that is no longer afforded to people in times of a pandemic. Unfortunately, mass gatherings like weddings or anniversaries are going to have to be celebrated on another date or just cancelled altogether. There is a huge risk that the virus will be able to spread around very easily during mass gatherings like these. So, in the interests of peoples' general safety and security, public celebrations are to be put on hold until after the pandemic subsides.

## *Dealing with Mass Spectacles Like Concerts or Sporting Events*

It's not just personal celebrations and gatherings that have to be put on hold when there's an epidemic going on. If a wedding of 300 people poses a very serious health risk for attendees, think about how dangerous it would be to hold a sporting event with more than 20,000 people crammed together in a small space. These kinds of events would be cesspools for disease and viruses. Music festivals, concerts, basketball games, Broadway shows, and other such mass gatherings are likely to be suspended while the pandemic is in full force.

## *Dealing with Religious or Spiritual Gatherings*

Another major way in which people might have to really adjust the way that they live is with their religious practices. It's typical for most religions to take at least one day in the week and gather as one community. Christians gather in churches, Muslims gather in mosques, Buddhists gather in monasteries, and so on. Again, these kinds of mass gatherings are to be greatly discouraged in the middle of a pandemic. A lot of people might be hesitant to give up their religious practices. However, this is a necessary measure to suppress the spread of the virus.

### *Going to Markets and Stores to Pick Up Daily Essentials*

Of course, no one expects you to be able to survive for an extended period of time by just locking yourself up in your house or condo. Eventually, your basic necessities are going to run out and you will have to replenish your supplies. This necessitates the need for you to head out and visit markets or stores to buy your essentials. In this sense, it's an absolute necessity as access to these basic needs are essential to your survival.

Given that, going to markets and stores must still be undertaken with utmost care and sensitivity. Ideally, only one person per household would be in charge of picking up these necessities so that social distancing is still practiced properly. Also, avoid human interaction while you're out and about as much as possible. The less time you expose yourself to other people, the better. It's not just about protecting yourself. It's also about protecting others just in case you happen to be a carrier of the virus without your knowing. When you restrict your movements, it's going to bode better for efforts in curbing the pandemic.

## Remaining Civil and Reasonable

Now, social interactions don't just concern themselves with public outings and mass gatherings. Social conduct in terms of communicating with others is also going to be just as important when it comes to maintaining order during a pandemic.

Obviously, you aren't going to be interacting with too many people in person when there's a pandemic going on. However, given that we live in the age of information and social media, dialogue and communication through digital platforms are still very helpful in staying connected.

We've already established that a pandemic is a crisis. And during times of crisis, there is a tendency for people to get swept up in all of the hysteria that comes along with it. This can be very dangerous as hysteria can induce unreasonable and irrational thought. This is how fake news and misinformation gets spread around.

People act on impulse by sharing random communications with one another without verifying or analyzing this information beforehand.

On top of that, a pandemic is a very tense and sensitive situation. People will have a tendency to panic and act emotionally. These emotions can often lead people to say things that are either offensive or just downright hurtful. Sometimes, there are certain things that need to be said even though they might come off as hurtful. However, a lot of the time, people just spread hate messages without any reason other than to add to the pandemonium. So, you are going to have to expect a lot of discussions that you may deem to be less than civilized and reasonable.

### Engaging in Respectful and Proper Dialogue

When you push people into a corner and they find themselves in rather desperate situations, there is a good chance that they will respond with desperation as well. However, this desperation might be ill-placed and may be potentially doing more harm than good. For example, if a local government imposes a lockdown on a certain area to prevent the spread of a virus indefinitely, certain people aren't going to be happy with it. During the initial implementation of restrictions, they might cooperate. However, if there are certain households who are stuck without jobs or any sources of income, this might generate a certain air of discontent and displeasure with the imposition of a lockdown. And when the levels of discontent and displeasure get too high, expect certain people to articulate their grievances accordingly.

These grievances might be valid and they might not. However, all of this noise can only add to the tension of the discourse in the community.

## Fighting Prejudices and Discrimination

There is also a matter of prejudices and discrimination. When people are put in rather inconvenient positions even though it isn't their fault, they are going to want to find someone to blame. People will look for a scapegoat.

This is where prejudices and discrimination might come in. For example, if you look back at previous and more recent pandemics that originated in China, you will see all of the immediate discrimination on full display; a lot of people will falsely attribute the fault to the entire Chinese population.

But it's not just that. Whenever the virus starts breaking out into other countries or communities, the blame game intensifies even further. Communities will blame the sources of the virus in their vicinity and might even vilify them.

Keep in mind that a lot of these initial carriers don't realize that they are infected to begin with. On top of that, they are dealing with a sickness while they are being vilified by the general public. This is a very real and probable occurrence for any community in a pandemic state. Whether that kind of hysteria is warranted or not is up to you.

# Final Thoughts

If there's one thing that we can't afford to lose in a time of crisis, it's our humanity. It's very important that even when things get really disastrous and dire, you are still able to cling onto your sense of social responsibility. After all, a pandemic is not an issue that can be resolved on its own or by just a select group of people. The only way to really suppress or even kill off a pandemic is if all people of the world decide to join forces and band together. Ultimately, it should be that kind of commitment to social responsibility that inspires and motivates us to overcome the struggles that come with a pandemic

This is why it takes a pooled commitment of the entire global population. It has to be a systemic effort that surpasses those of a mere individual. This is also why it's important for people to always remain cordial and respectful.

When faced with a grave threat, we can't afford to be bickering among ourselves and generating unnecessary tension. There is already enough tension to go around during a pandemic as it is.

Social life is going to change as a result of a pandemic. You can be certain of that fact even though a pandemic tends to bring with it a lot of uncertainty. So, just because social dynamics have to change in such dramatic degrees doesn't mean that it has to change for the worse. In fact, that should be a call for us as human beings to be more mindful of the way that we conduct ourselves in relation to other people. We have to be more sensitive during a pandemic of what kind of repercussions our words and actions can have on the people around us.

We have to remember that, at the end of the day, everyone is going through the same kind of struggle as you are. However, while these struggles may not differ so much by kind, they can definitely differ by degrees. Not everyone is going to be going to have it as hard as you. Not everyone is going to be as privileged or blessed as you. It's all relative. However, there is one common threat here, and it's the pandemic. So, more than anything else, all efforts should be directed towards solving that crisis, whether directly or indirectly.

## CHAPTER 5:

# How do we Adapt to an Ever-Changing World?

As any reasonable person might suspect, merely living through and surviving a pandemic is not enough. That's only half the job. Sure, there is a cause for celebration if you are able to survive a pandemic. But the job is definitely not done. Just because you manage to make it through a pandemic unscathed doesn't mean that you are going to forever be immune to it. That's not how pandemics work. As evidenced by history, pandemics are naturally occurring phenomenon in the world. There are millions of little viruses and bacteria that roam the world every day and are invisible to the naked eye. At some point, another rare disease-causing virus is going to materialize and potentially bring about a global pandemic again. This is why, in the principles of adaptability and survival, human civilization is able to prepare for pandemics in the future.

It's always best that we take a proactive, rather than reactive approach to solving a pandemic. This is the absolute best way to minimize the depth of catastrophe that may arise from the emergence of a pandemic. They say that the best defense is a good offense. This is essentially what being proactive is. Instead of waiting to act once an outbreak materializes, it's important that people devote more of their time and efforts into preparing for the next one. Rather than focusing all of the information on this book on how to make it through a pandemic, you are also going to be briefed on what happens after.

This chapter is going to try to talk about what life should be like in between pandemics. It's always about being able to see the bigger picture here. It should never just be about how you would survive every pandemic each time they come along. It's also about how the human species will be able to survive pandemic states in the long-term. We want to mitigate the damage as much as possible. And the most effective means of doing so would be through proper preparation and anticipation. Granted, it's very difficult to talk about concrete steps moving forward. However, there are some general principles that we can use and keep to heart.

Remember that the whole theme of this book is adaptability. Obviously, when the world is faced with a grave threat like a pandemic, it's important that society is able to adjust in order to minimize the likelihood of that threat returning. At the very least, being adaptable would entail people and institutions be better prepared for these threats when they come so that damages are minimized as much as possible. So, with that, here are a few principles that we might want to keep in mind as we look forward to life after a pandemic.

## Learning from History

Again, pandemics are not new. There have been numerous pandemics that have happened over the course of history. Countless civilizations that have preceded us have been exposed to all sorts of diseases and outbreaks. However, if you go back to the earliest epochs of human existence, people really didn't have to worry about global pandemics. Back then, human beings were very tribal and territorial. This means that they rarely ever ventured outside of their communities. This means that any outbreaks that might have taken place rarely ever infected neighboring communities.

However, we all know that to no longer be the case today. The dramatic shift took place when trade and travel started becoming rampant practices in various civilizations.

Eventually, human beings started to visit nearby villages, towns, and cities as the world began to modernize. Once cohabitation with different communities became a possibility, containing contagious diseases became all the more difficult. We already briefly touched on the history of pandemics in a previous chapter of this book. Now, if we are able to understand how our ancestors dealt with their pandemics in the past, then we would be placing ourselves in better positions to deal with pandemics in the future.

For a huge bulk of human history, sanitation and cleanliness have always been major issues. Even today, numerous highly urbanized areas struggle to maintain sanitary conditions, especially in places where poverty is rampant.

In this modern age, one of the most common culprits for breeding diseases are in unsanitary places like open sewers, factories for animal proteins that are very poorly maintained, and in impoverished areas where citizens don't have ample running water or toilet facilities.

If you compare the earliest human civilizations to the one we have today, they definitely had it a lot easier. It was much simpler a task for them to deal with disease outbreaks since they were much more isolated than we are today. However, when globalization's wheels started turning, various global health crises also began to come to life. One of the most prominent pandemics in all of history was the one that impacted the Byzantine Empire in the mid-sixth century. Historians and researchers identified the pathogen as Yersinia pestis. However, these days, it's more popularly known as the Bubonic plague. It was a pathogen that was originally carried by rats and made its way into humans through fleas.

The fleas would serve as the carriers of the disease and jump from rats to human beings. Keep in mind, though, that during this time, humans had not yet learned about germs (bacteria and viruses), and how diseases were spread between people.

The plague first started in Egypt, but eventually made its way to Constantinople (now Istanbul) through ships carrying wheat and grains. At that time, Constantinople was one of the most advanced and populous civilizations in the world. Naturally, it didn't take long for the outbreak to reach dramatic heights. Based on estimates of historians, more than 5,000 people were dying every single day. By the time the pandemic started to diminish, more than half the population of Europe had been eliminated by the disease; almost 100 million people.

Unfortunately, as sad as that event might have been, it was not the last time that human beings would have to face that plague. More than 800 years later, the Bubonic plague made its comeback and managed to cause even more catastrophe the second time around. Many consider this second round of the Bubonic plague to be the most notorious pandemic in all of human history. It first originated in late 1347 when a ship that was docked at a port in Sicily had been filled with sailors who were experiencing some very mysterious symptoms. These people were definitely ill as they had exhibited dark swells in their armpit and groin areas. Due to the appearance of these swells, the plague later went on to be known as the Black Plague or the Black Death. From that boat, the disease would eventually spread rapidly all across the continent, killing almost half of its population, again, along the way.

One of the biggest mistakes that people at that time had made in an effort to suppress the plague was turning to religion. These days, when an outbreak takes place, there are some serious protocols that are implemented such as quarantines and social distancing measures. Many individuals then take hand washing and sanitizing very seriously. People will typically start to wear masks whenever they need to go out or interact with others.

However, this was not normal behavior for people back then. In fact, far from it. Instead of taking some very practical medical and sanitary measures to curb the spread of disease, people turned to prayer. Europe at that time was a hotbed for Christianity. Many saw the plague as God's wrath and sought to engage in penitence in order to appease the situation. They would gather in large groups, not knowing yet about germ-theory, and unknowingly spreading the disease to their neighbors, family members and friends.

However, that isn't to say that European governments at that time didn't enforce any policies to try to prevent the plague from spreading. There were also some quarantine-like policies that were implemented during that time. Italy had banned sailors from traversing or entering key ports for around a month. However, the government would later on decide to extend the banning of transients to a total of 40 days. In Italian, 40 days literally translates to quaranta giorni. This Italian translation of "40 days" would later evolve to become the English word "quarantine."

It was a trial and error process for human beings over the millennia. As people grew more and more knowledgeable about disease, the better equipped we have become in dealing with outbreaks. We have now acquired much more profound understandings of disease transmissions, vaccines, and sanitary measures to minimize the likelihood of outbreaks in the first place. Vaccines have been especially useful in helping people become immune to one of the most prominent illnesses known to man: the common flu.

There's this old adage that says, "those who fail to study history are doomed to repeat it." Fortunately, that hasn't been the case for us so far when it comes to handling outbreaks and diseases (for the most part). Nowadays, we have much more knowledge and resources to help us treat various diseases compared to what people in the past had at their disposal. It's very unlikely that any new or emerging pandemic will create the same kind of havoc that the Spanish Flu or the Black Death used to have on society. These days, it's just a matter of making sure that we never grow complacent. Sure, we have been on the right track so far, but there is still so much to do moving forward.

In all likelihood, people are still going to panic should a pandemic arise. But that panic isn't always a bad thing. To a certain extent, it's that kind of fear that can lead people to be more proactive and measured in their approaches to dealing with the pandemic in the first place. However, we have to be very careful to not let this slight panic evolve into mass hysteria. That would only end up making matters a lot worse. When crisis strikes, it's important that community leaders step up and set the proper course moving forward to ensure the safety and protection of the general public. However, it's also just as important that individuals take sensible efforts to keep themselves aware of accurate and reputable information, and to make sure that everyone is alert and updated on emerging matters.

## Strengthening the Economy

Sometimes, when a pandemic gets drawn out a little too long. An economy can suffer vastly. We've already discussed this topic in a previous chapter. You might already be familiar with the best economic practices to undertake while a pandemic is going on. However, what do you do to the economy once the pandemic has subsided? Is it just business as usual or do more drastic steps need to be undertaken in order to ensure the safety of the global economy?

Well, for one, more funding should be devoted to health and medical research in order to prepare medical frontliners better. Also, government welfare should be readily available to not just help keep individual families afloat, but also small businesses as well. The flow of money during a pandemic is always going to be compromised. This is why certain economic practices and policies should be enacted in between pandemics to make sure that the entire economy doesn't collapse from being in a pandemic state.

Also, on a grassroots level, individuals should take better care to be more mindful of their finances. Emergency funds should always be readily available in times of crises. Usually, people associate emergency funds with getting fired or getting sick. However, not many people think about needing emergency funds in a pandemic state since these events don't happen all that often.

## Anticipating and Preventing the Next Pandemic

Ultimately, to be blunt about it, the key to preventing future pandemics is in realizing and acknowledging the causes of previous pandemics. In more recent history, most of the influenza viruses that have managed to induce pandemics originated in wet markets, or live animal markets found throughout the world. The reason these wet markets are common sources of disease is because so many living organisms are living in close proximity, within extremely unhygienic conditions. When that's the case, it's very easy for bacteria to grow and mutate from one animal to another. Eventually, this disease-causing bacteria might latch onto a human host and ignite the start of an impending pandemic.

So, it should be obvious that one of the biggest ways to ensure the safety of the general public moving forward is to impose stricter regulations on the conduct of these wet markets. At the very least, if these wet markets are to continue with their existence, they should have better standards for sanitation and hygiene moving forward. While certain economies might take a hit as a result of closing or regulating wet markets, it's nothing compared to the worldwide economic hit of dealing with the fallouts of a pandemic.

In addition to that, governments should also make sure to strengthen their protocols and policy reviews in anticipation of the next pandemic. Proper information dissemination and policy enforcement mechanisms should be polished prior to the arrival of any outbreak. Government institutions are always in the best positions to enforce mass mobilization efforts to keep people safe and protected from contagious diseases. Common protocols such as travel bans and community quarantines should definitely be mainstays when dealing with early stages of a pandemic.

## Final Thoughts

It can be very difficult to anticipate how the future is going to turn out. However, that shouldn't be an excuse for us to not think about how we can best prepare for possible crises. It should be in everyone's best interests to always do their parts in making sure that they prepare themselves for the future.

Whether you're talking about large-scale medical institutions, government offices, or individual families, everyone should be taking proactive measures when it comes to dealing with pandemics.

As history has taught us, disease outbreaks are very serious. Also, they might even be inevitable. Until it gets to a point wherein medical professionals are able to develop a magical vaccine that will render everyone on earth immune to any kind of contagious disease, we are all vulnerable. And, honestly, that's unlikely since organisms, as we first mentioned, will continue to evolve to assure their survival. Instead of hoping on a magic vaccine, we should try our best to minimize our vulnerability by arming ourselves with adequate knowledge and information to combat diseases moving forward.

This is truly what it means to survive in this world. This is what it means to be fit. It's not just about being able to withstand tough trials while we are in them. It's also about being smart and methodical. It's about making sure that we minimize our exposure to these kinds of crises as much as possible. As they say in the medical community, prevention is better than cure.

**CHAPTER 6:**

# Summary

A lot of concepts have been covered in this book so far and it's okay if you're feeling overloaded with information at this point. After all, pandemics are not simple matters. They require a lot of study, analysis, review, and reflection. Naturally, your brain might be a little bit exhausted by all of the reading that you've been doing so far. So, given that, it might be a good idea to concisely rehash all of the vital information that was covered in this book. Consider this final chapter to be the act of you coming full circle with everything that you've learned up to this point.

# What is Social Distancing?

Social distancing is essentially the art of establishing as much physical distance between yourself and other people as much as possible. So, this means that there should be a large-scale prohibition of mass gatherings in public. As much as possible, people should be staying at home and quarantining themselves during a pandemic.

This is the most effective method in preventing the spread of the disease and in flattening the curve. There are certain people out there who might be asymptomatic even though they are infected by a contagious disease. In these instances, they might not feel sick, but they are serving as carriers of the disease. And this disease might potentially be fatal to the people these carriers come into contact with.

So, with social distancing, you are lessening the chances of you being infected by a disease. Also, you are lessening the chances of you infecting other people with the diseases should you be a carrier.

## What is "Flattening the Curve?"

Flattening the curve is essentially a phrase that is used to represent the desires of the medical community to slow down the spread of a disease. The curve represents a line in a graph that curves more and more when numerous people are getting sick within a short span of time. To flatten the curve essentially means slowing down the spread of disease so that the number of people getting sick within a set period of time would lessen. This is especially important during pandemics when hospitals and other medical institutions can become overwhelmed with their patients. When society is able to flatten the curve during a pandemic, medical professionals are able to treat their patients in a more timely and wholesome manner without being overwhelmed. Over time, even though more and more people become infected with a disease, medical professionals are able to treat them better when they are more spread out over extended periods as opposed to all at once.

## How Should We Conduct Ourselves in a Pandemic State?

During a pandemic state, you should try to live as normal a life as possible while still adhering to the principles of social distancing. This means that you should still be making use of technology to interact with your friends and colleagues. It's important that you still take the time to take care of your health by eating nutritious food and exercising regularly. You should also be developing current talents or learning new skills. Also, if the nature of your occupation permits it, you should also be staying productive with your professional life while you're quarantining yourself.

# What are the Best Economic Practices During a Pandemic?

Work from home. Regardless if you are a business owner or an employee, you should always be staying at home. Of course, there are certain exceptions like medical practitioners or community leaders who have to stay at the frontlines. However, for the most part, professionals should be looking to stay at home and stay productive there. If the nature of your profession doesn't permit you to work from home, then consider finding alternate sources of income to keep you afloat. Manage your money properly and make sure that this pandemic doesn't put you into a state of financial ruin. Also, don't be afraid of maximizing whatever government support or aid you can get.

## What are our Responsibilities to Society in a Pandemic?

You have a duty to not be stubborn and selfish in times of a pandemic. So, while it may be tempting to push through with a wedding or a birthday party, don't. You owe it to yourself and the people around you to adhere to the principles of social distancing as much as possible. Also, be very wary of the way that you express yourself and communicate with others. Do not allow the mass hysteria of a pandemic to get the best of you. Be vigilant of any misinformation or fake news that is spreading around. Also, be a bastion for responsible information gathering and data sharing.

# What are the Best Measures we can Take to Prepare for Future Pandemics?

For the most part, it's really all about learning from history. In order to better prepare ourselves for future pandemics, we have to look at past outbreaks and how we responded to them. Implement the best practices from the previous outbreaks and build upon them. Acknowledge the mistakes in dealing with previous outbreaks and make sure to never commit them again in the future. By looking into the past, we will be in a better position to arm ourselves against threats in the future.

# Conclusion

It's a truly scary time whenever a pandemic overtakes the world. There is a good chance that the world will never go back to the way that it once was prior to the start of a pandemic. For a lot of people, there is a matter of dealing with lost loved ones as a result of succumbing to illnesses. During a pandemic, it's so easy to throw around statistics and data out there documenting the number of people who are affected or who have succumbed to the disease. However, what most people fail to realize is that these statistics are more than just numbers.

These numbers represent actual people whose lives have been changed or have been taken away from them altogether. And when these people die from a disease, they are leaving behind people who love them and will miss them until their time will come. It's so easy to get lost in all of the hysteria of a pandemic to the point that we fail to see the humanity in it. There are people who lose the battle physically and to them, the world as they once knew it is gone forever.

But there is also the matter of rebuilding humanity and the systems that comprise it. Businesses, medical institutions, and government institutions might have to also rebuild themselves in an effort to recapture what life was like prior to the pandemic. Obviously, this is no easy feat. Depending on how broad the reach and influence of a pandemic, it can take a very long time for certain communities and societies to build themselves back up again.

Naturally, a pandemic is no laughing matter and people always need to take it seriously. A pandemic can serve as a potent threat against the human species as a whole. As has been previously discussed, these natural threats come and go, and it's up to us to deal with them whenever they make their moves. As a human being, it's absolutely vital that you arm yourself with the knowledge and the information that is necessary to increase your chances of survival during a pandemic. And it's not just about merely preserving life that we're talking about here. It's also a matter of preserving the quality of life.

Not everyone is always going to be able to predict when the next big pandemic is going to hit. There is a good chance that a virus could break out and affect numerous people and countries all over the world in the blink of an eye. If a pandemic is strong enough, it will be able to crush economies and test the strength of the world's health-care systems. People will find themselves in isolation, unable to cope with life in a pandemic state. Pandemics will disrupt the way that modern society functions in ways that we might not ever be able to imagine. A pandemic with big enough power and influence can forever taint a person's psyche.

There are health experts and scientists who say that a truly devastating global pandemic is inevitable. All around the world, there are seasoned professionals and reputable sources who claim that the world is going to have to scramble to put out the fires of the next big one. If you put it that way, it can feel like we have lost all hope as human beings. If the next devastating pandemic is truly inevitable, then what else is there for us to do? Should we merely put our arms down and allow the tragedy to take place? Well, not necessarily.

As much as possible, we have to operate with the assumption that the human civilization is going to live on. So, regardless if we're dealing with health crises now or if we're anticipating the big ones that have yet to come, it's important that we really take the time to prepare ourselves accordingly. And you're already taking that first step by reading materials such as this one. This is definitely a good sign. But it has to be a concerted effort among a significantly large group of individuals. Dealing with a global pandemic is going to require the unified effort of the whole world.

As a species, we have faced many great threats all throughout history. Some of those threats happen to be pandemics. These naturally (and sometimes, unnaturally) occurring health crises are nothing new. They have been around for as long as we've been able to keep tabs on history. However, another thing that isn't new is the human ability to overcome adversity. We have proven time and time again that we have the capacity to beat these threats away to preserve our place in the world. We've proven as a species that we are fit to survive and that we know how to deal with these threats no matter how grave they might be.

So, as much as possible, take all of the necessary measures and precautions possible to ensure that we are equipped to handle the next big pandemic. And when that time comes, maintain that hope and belief in yourself and in those around you. No matter how difficult things might seem when the time comes, you must stay confident in your ability to overcome these obstacles in the face of adversity. At that point, human resilience can be your greatest ally and you must use it to your advantage.

Hopefully, this book will have provided you a lot of pragmatic insights into how you would be able to survive a pandemic and emerge into a new world. But more than that, hopefully, this book will have given you the confidence, determination, and strength to know that you have what it takes to face a big health crisis like a pandemic head on. A new world is up for the taking after the pandemic is over. You just have to make sure that you're still there for it when the time comes.